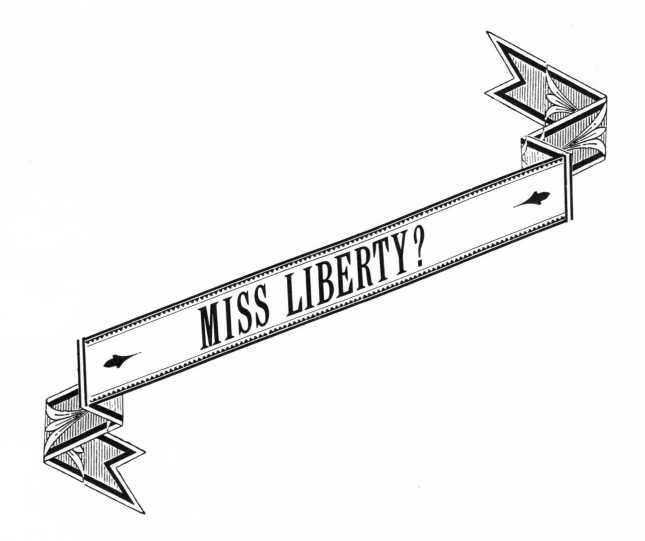

So stands the statue that enchants the world.
　　　　　　　　　　　—*James Thomson*

MISS LIBERTY?

71
collages by
John Digby

THAMES AND HUDSON

First published in the United States in 1986 by Thames and Hudson Inc., 500 Fifth Avenue, New York, New York 10110
First published in Great Britain in 1986 by Thames and Hudson Ltd, London

Library of Congress Catalog Card Number 84-72571

Designed by Janet Doyle
Printed in the United States of America

A very special note of thanks must be given to my wife, Joan, who read innumerable speeches, political papers, poems, and books in order to find these texts on liberty. Without her involvement and work I doubt whether the book would have been completed.

Puritanism, believing itself quick with the seeds of religious liberty,
laid without knowing it the egg of democracy.
—*James Russell Lowell*

Liberty, *noun*. One of Imagination's most precious possessions.
　　　　　　　　　　　　　　　　　　　　—*Ambrose Bierce*

He that commands the sea is at great liberty.
—*Francis Bacon*

The greatest dangers to liberty lurk in
insidious encroachments by zealous men.
—*Louis Dembitz Brandeis*

O Liberty! forgive the base endeavour.
—*Percy Bysshe Shelley*

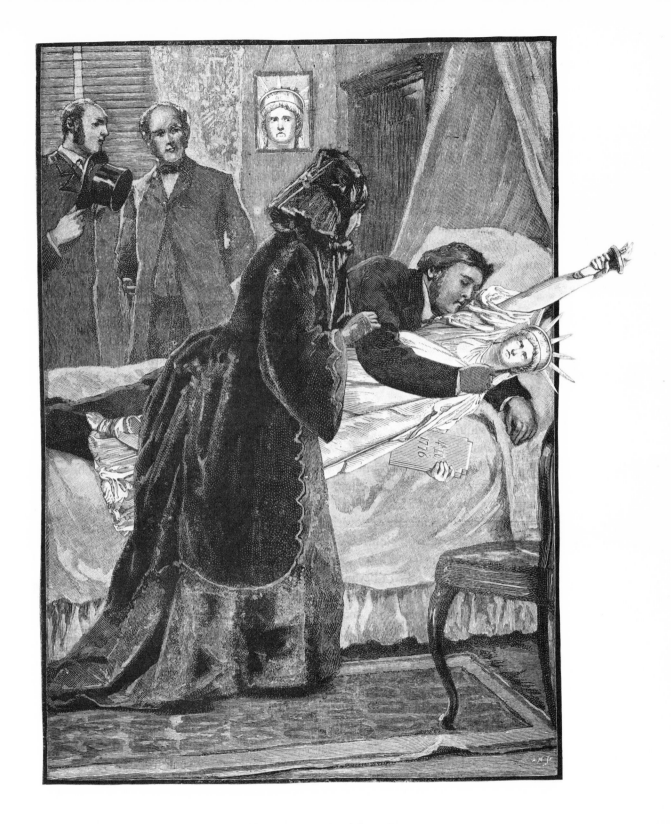

We are not to expect to be translated from despotism
to liberty in a featherbed.

—*Thomas Jefferson*

Liberty exists in proportion to wholesome restraint.
—*Daniel Webster*

What more felicity can fall to creature,
Than to enjoy delight with liberty.
——*Edmund Spenser*

15

If I have freedom in my love,
And in my soul am free,
Angels alone that soar above,
Enjoy such liberty.
—*Richard Lovelace*

In the contest between ease and liberty,
the first hath generally prevailed.
—*George Savile,*
First Marquess of Halifax

The disease of liberty is catching.
—*Thomas Jefferson*

O Liberty! with profitless endeavor
Have I pursued thee, many a weary hour.
—*Samuel Taylor Coleridge*

I do not desire liberty to choose windbags and
nincompoops to represent me in Parliament.
—*George Bernard Shaw*

People confound liberty of thinking with liberty of talking.
—*James Boswell*

Without knowledge, could your fathers have conquered liberty?
—*Frances Wright*

The tree of liberty only grows when watered
by the blood of tyrants.
——*Bertrand Barère de Vieuzac*

The cost of liberty is less than the price of repression.
—*W. E. B. Du Bois*

The liberty here enjoyed by the young women
often occasions some surprise to foreigners.
—*Frances Wright*

More liberty begets desire of more;
The hunger still increases with the store.
—*John Dryden*

It is true that liberty is precious—
so precious that it must be rationed.
—*attributed to Lenin*

The hungry and the homeless don't care about liberty any more than they care about cultural heritage. To pretend that they do care is cant.

—*E. M. Forster*

. . . shewing how Commerce on Liberty thrives.
—*George Gordon, Lord Byron*

29

As technology has advanced in America, it has increasingly encroached on one of those liberties—what I term the right of personal privacy.
—*Richard M. Nixon*

That night he has his arms at liberty.
—*William Congreve*

Yf I nowe had her at my liberte I sholde make her to deye a cruell deth.
—*William Caxton*

Liberty is dangerous, as hard to live with as it is elating.
—*Albert Camus*

I must have liberty
Withal, as large a charter as the wind
To blow on whom I please.
—*William Shakespeare*

Inequality is as dear to the American heart as liberty itself.
—*William Dean Howells*

Animated by the presence of liberty, they began their operations.
—*James Thomson*

. . . give me liberty or give me death.
—*Patrick Henry*

Where liberty dwells . . .

. . . there is my country.
　　　　　　　　—*Cato*

Even liberty itself is bartered here.
—*Oliver Goldsmith*

What has the Wretch that has survived his Country,
His Friends, his Liberty, to hazard?
                —*Samuel Johnson*

What did you do, revolutionaries frightened of revolution,
political tricksters, buffoons of liberty?

—*Alexander Herzen*

. . . the shortest way for a tyrant to get rid of
a troublesome champion of liberty. . . .
　　　　　　　　　　　—*George Bernard Shaw*

Millions of women are asserting their right to voluntary motherhood. . . .
It is for woman the key to the temple of liberty.

—*Margaret Sanger*

He who would save liberty must put his trust in democracy.
—Norman Thomas

We have other trenches, in fact, to overcome with the cry of "liberty."
—*François Mitterand*

Such charms has death when join'd with liberty.
—*Alexander Pope*

47

With what deep worship I have still adored
The spirit of divinest Liberty.
—*Samuel Taylor Coleridge*

Virtue and Liberty engross his soul.
—*Samuel Johnson*

The true liberty of a man, you would say, consisted in his finding out,
or being forced to find out, the right path and walk thereon.
—*Thomas Carlyle*

Delight and liberty, the simple creed
Of Childhood.
                    —*William Wordsworth*

. . . a new nation, conceived in Liberty. . . .
—*Abraham Lincoln*

Plainly the sheep and the wolf are not agreed upon a definition of liberty.
—*Abraham Lincoln*

What are the Rights of Man and the Liberties of the World but Loose-Fish?
—*Herman Melville*

We can hope, then, in regard to what constitutes the material
and the manner of art, for a liberty of unimaginable opulence.
—*Guillaume Apollinaire*

I'll be preparing myself to go out as a missionary to preach liberty
to them that are enslaved—your harem inmates among the rest.
—*Charlotte Brontë*

Brightest in dungeons, Liberty! thou art.
—*George Gordon, Lord Byron*

. . . graver hours, that bring constraint
To sweeten liberty.
                              —*Thomas Gray*

She gazed . . . on the sullen, surging waters that lay between her and liberty.
—*Harriet Beecher Stowe*

. . . a great race of women . . .

. . . who could look liberty in the face.
—Emma Goldman

The cause of liberty becomes a mockery if the price to be paid
is the wholesale destruction of those who are to enjoy liberty.
—*Mohandas K. Gandhi*

He loves to sit and hear me sing,
    Then, laughing, sports and plays with me;
Then stretches out my golden wing,
    And mocks my loss of liberty.
                    —*William Blake*

Moses and Aaron were to assure Pharaoh that God sent them and they were in His name to demand liberty for the Children of Israel.

—Daniel Defoe

If any should doubt the effect produced by the infringement of female liberty upon the female mind, let them consider the dress of the present generation of English women.
—*Frances Wright*

Our joint love of liberty was spawned by a common heritage.
—*toast of Ronald Reagan to Margaret Thatcher*

To set upon one battle all our liberties.
—*William Shakespeare*

We have buried the putrid corpse of liberty.
—*Benito Mussolini*

The ground of liberty must be gained by inches.
—*Thomas Jefferson*

Liberty don't work as good in practice as it does in speech.
—*Will Rogers*

Liberty is given by nature even to mute animals.
—*Tacitus*

But see! where Liberty, on yonder strand,
Where the cliff rises, and the billows roar,
Already takes her melancholy stand,
To wing her passage to some happier shore.
                              —*Thomas Chatterton*

Abstract liberty, like other mere abstractions, is not to be found.
—*Edmund Burke*

The liberty of the artist is art's finest illusion.
—*John Digby*

The God who gave us life, gave us liberty at the same time.
—*Thomas Jefferson*

Their liberty belongs to them.
—*Jean Jacques Rousseau*

Hail, Liberty! Hail!
—*Dionysios Solomos*